The **Essential** Buyer's Guide

ROVER

2000, 2200 & 3500

All P6 models: 2000/2200 SC & TC,
Three Thousand Five, 3500 & 3500S 1963 to 1977

Your marque expert:
Martyn Marrocco

T0386221

VELOCE PUBLISHING
THE PUBLISHER OF FINE AUTOMOTIVE BOOKS

www.veloce.co.uk

First published in July 2019 by Veloce Publishing Limited, Veloce House, Parkway Farm Business Park, Middle Farm Way, Poundbury, Dorchester DT1 3AR, England. Tel +44 (0)1305 260068 / Fax 01305 250479 / e-mail info@veloce.co.uk / web www.veloce.co.uk or www.velocebooks.com.

ISBN: 978-1-787113-77-0; UPC: 6-36847-01377-6

Introduction
– the purpose of this book

The Rover P6 – P6 standing for the sixth postwar production model – was launched as the 'Rover 2000' in October 1963 to world-wide acclaim. It was arguably the most technologically advanced and innovative production car ever made in the UK, even the world.

Its construction centred around a sturdy, steel base frame to which all mechanical units, and the steel and aluminium body panels, were bolted. This steel 'cage' made the car very strong in the event of an accident, and was one of many safety features built into the design of the car.

Suspension design was quite revolutionary for a production car, the rear boasting a de Dion tube arrangement that gave excellent road holding for the time. The front suspension was equally unusual: it had a cantilever arrangement operating horizontal road springs that, as well as offering an excellent ride, allowed extra room in the engine compartment, which meant that a variety of engines could be accommodated. Not least of these was the gas turbine unit that Rover engineers had been experimenting with for some time, although this never actually appeared on production models.

The styling of the bodywork and interior were cutting edge for the time, and gave Rover a new corporate image overnight, a huge departure from the rather staid, gentlemanly carriages it had produced previously. Times were changing, this was the start of the 'swinging sixties,' and Rover stepped up to the rapidly changing market brilliantly. The Rover 2000 was a smash hit; demand soon outstripped supply by two to one, and the factory worked around the clock to try and keep up.

The only power unit available on launch was the all-new, 2-litre, overhead cam, four-cylinder engine that was mated to a manual gearbox, which was also newly designed for the car. In 1967, an automatic transmission was offered for the 2000, and a twin carburettor model was also launched, known as the 2000TC (manual transmission only). In 1968, the all-aluminium, 3.5-litre V8 engine was installed into the P6 bodyshell creating the 'Three Thousand Five,' all of these were automatics. The 3500S was introduced in 1969, for export to the USA only; this was also fitted with an automatic gearbox. However, in 1971, a 'new' 3500S model replaced it. The 3500S was equipped with a manual gearbox, and was also available to other markets, including the UK. The last change of power unit occurred in 1973, when the capacity of the four-cylinder engines increased to 2.2 litres, with the models known as 2200SC and 2200TC. Production finally ended in 1977.

Owning a P6 today is like owning a piece of motoring history. Its light and airy cabin is just as pleasant now as it was when the car was launched in 1963. The seats are comfortable, and visibility first class. One peculiarity to P6 interiors is the smell: a mix of Connolly leather and top quality carpet, it is quite unique. Rolls-Royces have it, but it is not quite the same as a P6 Rover.

Performance is brisk, even in single carburettor form, with the V8 models being particularly capable, especially when equipped with manual transmission, and these models are highly prized today.

The early cars have a strong following, as many prefer their purity of design; of these, the Three Thousand Five is the strong performer, but a 2000TC will just about keep up with it, and is, undoubtedly, the sportier drive, with its manual gearbox and eager four-cylinder engine.

There are, of course, things to watch out for when looking for a P6, each model having its own characteristics and foibles. The object of this book is to help you to decide which model of P6 is right for you. The Rover P6 is a quality machine irrespective of which power unit is fitted, as each offers a unique driving experience. The marque is well supported by, at the time of writing, two very good owners' clubs, both offering excellent help and advice to prospective buyers. Values are currently very reasonable considering the level of technology employed, but they are rising steadily as the charms of the P6 become more well known. Also, there are still plenty to choose from, as the survival rate is currently quite healthy, but early, pre-face-lift cars are becoming more scarce as the years pass by, so if you want one of these, now may well be the time to buy.

The Rover P6 was one of the most technologically advanced saloon cars of its day.

Contents

The Essential Buyer's Guide™ currency
At the time of publication a BG unit of currency "●" equals approximately
£1.00/US$1.29/Euro 1.15. Please adjust to suit current exchange rates.

1 Is it the right car for you?

Tall and short drivers

The Rover P6 was the first production car to have proper ergonomics built into its design; consequently, drivers of all sizes should find things comfortable behind the wheel. The steering column is adjustable, and the front seats have precise rake adjustment thanks to a unique clutch mechanism.

For the first time in a British car, the switches and controls were designed for ease of reach and operation.

Weight of controls

Most P6s were built without power assisted steering, making parking heavier going than you might be used to in a modern car, though not overly so.

All switches and controls are very simple and easy to use. Note the large, easy to read instruments in this Series II car.

Once on the move, however, the steering is light and precise. The cars that were equipped with the power option, usually late model V8s, were fitted with a smaller, leather-rim steering wheel, and are very pleasant to drive.

The gear change on manual transmission cars is particularly precise, with a short travel between gears. The clutch, too, is light and precise, meaning smooth progress between the gears.

Automatics use the popular Borg Warner type 35 gearbox and, latterly, the type 65. Both are easy to use in all conditions.

Will it fit in the garage?

Length	178.5in (454cm)
Width	66in (168cm)
Height	54.75in (139cm)
Ground clearance	6.5in (16.5cm)
Wheelbase	103.375in (262.5cm)
Front track	53.375in (135.5cm)
Rear track	52.5in (133.3cm)

Interior space

The P6 accommodates four adults in great comfort. However, whilst most saloon cars of the period would also facilitate a fifth passenger in the centre

The P6's interior is a very nice place to be, but there is no room in the rear for a fifth passenger.

of the rear seat, the Rover's individual, sculpted rear seats don't really allow for this.

There is generous storage space in the two drop-down bins, one on each side of the dash, and also a large flat surface on top of the dash, which should be equipped with a none-slip rubber mat.

Luggage capacity

The P6s boot was always considered inadequate, even by Rover management at the time, and three solutions were developed to alleviate this. The main issue was the space taken up by the spare wheel, which was stored upright in the left-hand side of the boot.

One idea was to lay the wheel flat on the boot floor and cover it with a folding false floor that could be bought as an accessory from your local Rover dealer. This worked fairly well, but it is an uncommon item today.

By far the most popular solution was to make use of the boot-mounted spare wheel kit, available as an optional extra from the dealer. This allowed the spare wheel to be bolted to the outside of the boot lid, protected by a waterproof cover (complete with embossed Rover motif). When the spare wheel was stowed in the boot, the mounting kit was replaced by an attractive badge on the boot lid.

The third solution was a specially designed roof rack, but this is rarely seen.

Usability

As far as old cars go, the Rover P6 is as reliable as they get, and this applies to all models. However, few, if any, are still used as daily drivers, such is the respect held for them by most owners these days. As with the majority of classic cars, the Rover P6 is more likely to be seen on the show field than down at the local supermarket, although there is no reason why you couldn't use one every day if the mileage and wear and tear don't bother you.

These drop-down bins are a clever way to add extra storage. There is one on each side of the dash.

The P6's boot was always considered inadequate, a situation which did not improve when the battery was also placed there on Series II models, as here.

Poor boot space was a problem for many P6 owners, resolved by the optional boot mounted spare wheel kit.

Parts availability

Parts availability for all models is currently surprisingly good, with several specialists holding a large amount of both new old stock or used spares. The P6 is also supported by two owners' clubs, and these can be an excellent source of parts – especially the rarer items.

eBay is also an excellent way to search world-wide for parts.

Parts cost

Most parts, both new and used, are very reasonably priced. However, based on supply and demand, some of the less common items – such as the boot mounted spare wheel badge – can achieve higher prices.

Insurance

Classic car policies can be applied to all P6 models, albeit with the usual mileage limitations.

Investment potential

Without a doubt, it is the V8 models that currently command the highest prices, especially the manual transmission 3500S cars. However, as values for these models rise, so do values of the four-cylinder cars.

The very early cars are highly prized amongst P6 followers, and the prices reflect their rarity.

From an investment point of view, it is likely to be immaculate V8 cars with low mileage that continue to perform strongly, with the 1963/64 cars also fairing well – although the latter is a niche market. Of the rest, Series I cars will always be in demand, as there are fewer survivors, and the Series II, four-cylinder cars bring up the rear.

The Series I interior, here on a Three Thousand Five ...

Foibles

The P6 is an extremely well-built and equally well-thought-out car, the basic layout of which didn't really change throughout production, testament to the forethought and design skills of the Rover engineers. There is little to complain about with a good P6.

Plus points

- Conservative, classy British styling
- Technically advanced
- Extremely comfortable
- Glorious V8 engine
- V8s and TCs are both strong performers
- Panel replacement is remarkably easy

Minus points

- Four-cylinder engines are a little noisy when pushed
- Manual gearboxes can wear prematurely on V8s
- Rust in the base unit can be complex to repair
- Lack of power steering on many cars may not suit everyone

Alternatives

- Triumph 2000/2500
- Daimler 250 V8
- Jaguar Mk2 2.4-litre
- Volvo 144/164
- Ford Consul/Granada

... and here is the Series II interior; this time on a 3500S.

2 Cost considerations
– affordable, or a money pit?

Purchase price
At the time of writing, the cost of purchasing a good P6 is still very reasonable, especially considering how technically advanced it is.

The best Series I cars currently sell for around ●x8000-10,000, with the V8 automatic cars costing a little more (around ●x12,000).

Series II four-cylinder cars are more plentiful, and around ●x5000-8000 should buy you a really good one.

Series II V8s are undoubtedly the most sought after by most prospective purchasers, with manual transmission cars commanding a premium. Expect to pay around ●x10,000-13,000 for a good automatic, and over ●x15,000 for a comparable manual.

Naturally, cars needing work will be far cheaper than this, and show or concourse examples considerably more expensive.

Parts prices
• Brake calliper: ●x54-110
• Oil filter: ●x9.5
• Distributor cap: ●x5-10
• HT leads: ●x20
• Radiator: ●x165-185
• Water pump: ●x69-129
• Clutch kit: ●x89-138
• Alternator: ●x59-110
• Dynamo: ●x118
• Exhaust system (stainless steel): ●x365 (2000)/450 (V8)
• Front wing: ●x395
• Rear wing: ●x395
• Carpet set: ●x399
• Front bumper: ●x300
• Rear bumper: ●x400
• Over rider: ●x80

Servicing
All routine servicing should be within the capabilities of most home mechanics, with the possible exception of the rear brakes and de Dion tube, but these aren't so bad once you have done some research online and gained some tips.

The rear brakes are inboard discs with the callipers positioned awkwardly on top of the axle, this means that access is tight. However, the whole rear axle assembly can be dropped a few inches, which makes things a little easier.

All service parts are readily available.

Below is a general breakdown of the original factory recommended service schedule.

It should be noted that the sequence of normal maintenance attention repeats itself every 20,000 miles/32,000km:

All P6s are, for the most part, easy enough to service. This is a 2200TC.

Every 5000 miles/8000km
- Drain and refill engine sump, and, on twin carburettor models, the oil cooler.
- Renew engine oil filter.
- Replace air cleaner elements (2000TC models).
- Check carburettor slow running.
- Check oil in carburettor hydraulic damper(s).
- Check and clean sparkplugs. Gap 0.025in (0.60mm).

SC and automatic models:
- 9.0:1 compression ratio: Use only Champion N.9Y sparkplugs.
- 7.5:1 compression ratio: Use only Champion N.5 sparkplugs.

TC models:
- 9.0:1 compression ratio: Use only Champion N.6Y sparkplugs.
- 10.0:1 compression ratio: Use only Champion N.61 sparkplugs.
- Check distributor contact points. Gap 0.014-0.016in (0.35-0.40mm).
- Check water level in radiator or expansion tank.
- Check water level in screen washer reservoir.
- Lubricate dynamo. Oil hole at rear end of dynamo. Check gearbox oil level, top up if necessary to bottom of filler plug hole.
- Automatic transmission: The automatic gearbox oil level should be checked with engine idling and 'park' selected. Check fluid level, top up if necessary to 'full' mark on dipstick.
- Check final drive oil level, top up if necessary to bottom of filler plug hole.
- Check steering box adjustment, zero backlash without friction on steering wheel. Road wheels in straight-ahead position.
- Check that rubber boots on steering ball joints, ball swivels, radius rod and de Dion tube are not dislodged or damaged.
- Check fluid level in brake reservoir, top up if necessary to rib on filter.
- Check operation of brake reservoir level safety switch.
- Ignition 'on,' handbrake 'off,' unscrew and lift filler cap 1in (25mm); warning light should be illuminated.
- Check thickness of front and rear brake pads. Minimum thickness: Dunlop

0.25in (6mm); Girling, front 0.125in (3mm), rear 0.0625in (1.5mm) also check for oil contamination on brake cads and discs.

    Note – Handbrake has automatic adjuster; if handbrake lever movement is excessive check pad thickness, minimum 0.125in (3mm).

- Check fluid level in clutch reservoir, top up if necessary to bottom of filler neck.
- Check tyre pressures. Front: $26lb/in^2$ (1.8 kg/cm^2).
- Rear: 28 lb/in^2 (1.9 kg/cm^2). Inspect tyre treads.
- Lubricate propeller shaft sliding joint.
- Check battery acid level and specific gravity of electrolyte (unless maintenance free battery is fitted).
- Road test, carry out any adjustments required. Check operation of all lights and instruments. After test, check for oil, fuel or fluid leaks at all plugs, flanges, joints and unions. Check brake pipes and hoses for chafing or looseness.

Every 10,000 miles (16,000km)
As 5000 miles (8000km) plus:
- Clean and re-oil engine breather element.
- Clean diaphragm-type crankcase emission control as applicable.
- Replace air cleaner element, single and twin carburettor models.
- Replace sparkplugs. Gap 0.025in (0.60mm)

SC and automatic models:
- Clean and lubricate distributor.
- Check fan belt 0.31-0.44in (8-11mm) free movement when checked midway between dynamo and crankshaft pulleys.
- Check de Dion tube oil level, top up if necessary to bottom of filler plug hole.
- Check steering box oil level, top up if necessary to bottom of filler plug hole.
- Check front and rear hubs for leakage.
- Change round, wash and examine all road wheels for possible damage.
- Clean, grease and tighten battery terminals Check headlamp beam setting.
- Apply a few spots of oil to throttle linkage, handbrake linkage, door locks, etc. Do not allow oil to contaminate brake pads or discs.

Every 15,000 miles (24,000km)
Service as at 5000 miles (8000km).

Every 20,000 miles (32,000km)
As 5000 miles (8000km) and 10,000 miles (16,000km) but instead of checking gearbox and final drive unit oil levels Check tappet clearance, Drain and refill gearbox. Drain and refill final drive unit. Plus:
- Clean flame-trap type crankcase emission control, as applicable.
- Clean sediment bowl and filter on fuel pump. Check front wheel alignment, 0.0625in (1.5mm) toe-in plus or minus 0.0625 in (1.5mm). Note – The camber of the front wheels on this car is 0 degrees with a tolerance of plus or minus 1 degree. That is, the bottom of the wheels can splay out slightly.

    Remember, this is the original service schedule. After buying your P6, it would be wise to carry out the full 20,000 mile service first, as many of the items contained therein will probably not have been checked for many years.

All P6 models drive well enough to be used every day if desired, though this is not, perhaps, the fairest way to treat them. Modern vehicles can have a hard life (with the volume of traffic being what it is these days), which is probably why most P6s are reserved for occasional use now. Having said that, providing you don't mind racking up the miles, any P6 could be used as a daily driver.

With regards to performance, all models will keep up with modern traffic without issue, even on the motorway. Indeed, the V8 cars, especially manuals, will show many modern cars a clean pair of heels. The braking system

All P6s are supremely comfortable.

on all but the very earliest cars are first class, but even the early ones are still pretty good.

Economy isn't too bad, especially on 2000SC and 2200SC models, but don't expect the levels attained by manufacturers today. You may get up to 30mpg from a four-cylinder car and up to 20mpg from an eight-cylinder. On cars that only receive occasional use this isn't really an issue, but fuel costs can mount up if the car is used a lot, so bear this in mind.

The V8 engine can be a little thirsty, but offers strong performance.

Superbly built and incredibly stylish.

Many P6s don't have power steering, which may bother some people. However, non-assisted steering isn't so heavy going once on the move – only when parking can it become a little tiresome if you're not used to it. Realistically, it's part of the charm of driving an old car; fit all the mod cons, and it ceases to be old.

P6s are much admired on the road. Don't be surprised if, once parked up, you are inundated with people saying "my Granddad had one of those," or "my bank manager had one," which typifies the image of the P6: solid, reliable and stylish saloons for middle-class, British gentlemen. Nothing wrong with that!

One thing that can definitely make these cars stand out in today's traffic is the colours used on some models produced in the seventies. Rover came up with some unique and interesting hues, such as Paprika (orange) and Avocado (bright green). Although not for the shy and retiring, these bold colours were considered a modern and progressive move at the time.

The level of comfort is just as impressive today as it was when the P6 was first launched; there are few modern cars which are as comfortable as a Rover P6.

Good points
Very comfortable.
Adequate performance for modern traffic.
Reasonable economy.
Stylish image.
Spares availability surprisingly good.
Your bank manager will like you.

Bad points
Lack of power steering on some models.
Not much else.

4 Relative values
– which model for you?

At the time of writing, Rover P6s are still fairly plentiful, and the UK is the prime source, with values remaining sensible for the time being.

All factory-produced P6s were saloons, but around 160 estate conversions were carried out by FLM Panelcraft (in collaboration with Crayford) which were called the 'Estoura,' good examples of which can command high prices today.

The extremely rare P6 estate.

Another shot of the estate, this time from the rear.

Considered by many to be the purest P6, an early Series I 2000.

Modernised instrumentation was introduced on Series II cars.

Perhaps the first thing to consider when looking for a P6, is whether you want a Series I car or a later, Series II, face-lift version: both are visually different, although they drive more or less the same.

Many people favour the earlier cars with their plain flanks, unadorned by later trim and plastic grilles. By the same token, just as many prefer the Series II cars, with the typical seventies styling additions. It is simply a matter of personal taste. There are certainly more Series II cars around than Series Is. We shall come to engine choice later, but bear in mind there are no manual transmission V8 Series I cars, just automatics.

The Series II cars had revised interiors, the most notable of which is the instrumentation, which was very modern for its time. Front grilles were now made of plastic (with a not unattractive design), and bright rubbing strips were fitted all the way along the sides of the body. Twin power bulges were also incorporated into the bonnet pressing. These simple changes, along with other, minor detail differences, completely changed the image of the P6, making it appear much more modern and sporty. As far as face-lifts go, it was extremely successful.

Regarding trim levels: if you go for a Series I car, you have no choice, as they all came with the same (superbly comfortable) leather seats. Series II cars provided a choice of several different seat designs. The original seats were carried over from the Series I models on many cars, and these would sometimes be trimmed in brushed nylon, although this is rare. Some of the later cars had a new design of seat – the box pleat – that was available in leather, ribbed velour or, on very late cars, vinyl (labelled 'Ambla'). Two designs of headrest were available on all Series II P6s, one small and one large, and could be fitted on all four seats, though the design of the rears was different to the fronts.

Now we come to engines, and this makes a big difference to how a P6 performs. Series I cars were available with a 2-litre OHC four-cylinder engine, with either a single or twin SU carburettors (called the 'TC'), the difference in performance was marked, but a single carburettor car goes well enough. Note, however, that an automatic gearbox was never available on the TC model.

If you want more power, then you will need to search for a 3500 with a V8 engine, which suits the P6 very well, but remember that all Series I 3500s had an automatic gearbox.

Moving on to the Series II cars, these can be found with the 2-litre engine and, on later cars, a 2.2-litre unit, which both have a similar power output, but the latter has a little more torque. The same drivetrain issue applies to the 2200TC – no automatic option was ever available.

Series II V8s could be ordered with either the automatic gearbox, or with an uprated four-speed manual gearbox, the latter had quite sparkling performance, and was badged as a 3500S. Do not confuse this model to the Series I 3500S which was the North American-only option and had an automatic gearbox.

A few of the later Series I cars were fitted with power steering, but this is rare; far more Series IIs had it, but it was mainly fitted to the V8s, although it is a worthwhile option if you can find a car so equipped.

Regarding values: the burble of that V8 engine will always ensure a premium over the four-cylinder cars, and the same goes for the manual gearbox on the V8 models. However, the diminishing numbers of Series I cars mean that the value of these are increasing, meaning the price difference is reducing steadily.

Plastic grille featured on the Series II cars.

Another distinctive feature of the Series II cars was the addition of power bulges in the bonnet along with a new badge mounted on the front.

5 Before you view
– be well informed

To avoid a wasted journey – and the disappointment of the car not meeting your expectations – it will help if you make initial enquiries by email or a telephone call, and are clear about what questions you want to ask the seller before contacting them. So make a list. Some of the questions may appear basic and a matter of common sense, but it's surprising what you can forget to ask when you're engaged in conversation. You can also do your homework by checking the current price trends for that particular model.

Where is the car?
Unless you are lucky, you could well end up travelling some distance to see the car that you are interested in, so it isn't a bad idea to see some pictures before making the journey. In this day and age, most households have the facilities to take digital photographs, with even the average mobile phone taking excellent pictures. Ask the seller if they will email you some.

If the car is a considerable distance away, then consider the cost of getting it back home, especially if it needs work.

Dealer or private sale?
Buying from a reputable dealer has its advantages. He will have thoroughly checked out the car and should sell it with a warranty, so, although you might (but not necessarily) pay more than you would if it was a private seller, you are buying peace of mind. Also, the dealer will usually be happy to take the car back as a part exchange if you ever fancy a change.

Cost of collection and delivery
Do not underestimate the cost of having a vehicle properly transported on a truck or trailer. If you do decide to take this option, and it is often a good one, ensure the operative is experienced and properly insured to do the job; many aren't, sometimes resulting in disastrous consequences.

If you are buying a project car then having it professionally moved is essential, unless of course you can do it yourself with a trailer. However, there are good reasons for professional transportation, even if the car is a runner and 'on the road.' Quite often a P6 will have had limited use over several years, perhaps only attending shows in the summer months. A sudden long run can result in mechanical failures, sometimes serious ones. The usual culprits are the water pump, fuel pump or contact breaker/condenser/distributor cap. All of these will render your P6 helpless at the roadside. Don't take the risk, book a truck.

Of course, if you buy from a dealer the car will usually have been thoroughly checked over and probably serviced, making breakdowns far less likely. In the unlikely event that something does break the dealer will (should!) come out and fix it.

View – when and where
When viewing, try to avoid wet days (difficult in the UK), as rain on paintwork can, and usually does, hide many faults. If viewing in wet weather is unavoidable then be prepared and take along a leather or drying cloth.

Naturally, do not view a car in the dark unless, possibly, you know it is purely a project car, but even then it is not advisable.

Try to view the car outside or, at least, in a spacious, well-lit garage. A domestic garage will not allow you the space to view the car properly.

If buying from a dealer you may well be extended the luxury of viewing the car on a vehicle lift. This is, of course, very desirable.

Something many buyers don't pay enough attention to is the vehicle documents. Take your time to check these and don't, under any circumstances, be rushed into skimping on them by the seller.

Reason for sale

By all means ask why the car is for sale, but don't expect a totally honest answer. Remember, they want to sell the car! Of course, this doesn't apply to all sellers, just more than you might expect. Also, be cautious of owners who haven't had the car for very long. There may be a very good reason for this, but there may be a bad one too.

Many people stress how bad it is for a car to have a lot of owners, but this is not necessarily so. All P6s have been around for a long time, so a higher number of owners on the log book is quite common.

Also, the classic car market has changed in recent years. Some owners are habitual buyers who want to try many different makes and models, this means selling a car is necessary in order to make room for another. Many restorers do this, often moving a car on after restoration is complete. For them the thrill is in the restoration process, and a sale is needed to fund the next restoration.

Matching data/legal ownership

Check that all the documents relate to the vehicle you are looking at, it's surprising how many don't. Check the chassis number against the registration document and verify the MOT status of the vehicle.

It is unlikely that a P6 will be owned by a finance company, but it is possible. You can download a simple app on your smartphone to help in this respect, there are many to choose from such as *Vehicle Smart*, *Total Car Check* and *Vehicle Specs*.

Ensure you get a full and detailed receipt from the seller, including their name and address. You will be thankful for this if anything goes wrong.

DVSA 0300 123 9000   HPI 0845 300 8905   RAC 0800 015 6000
DVLA 0844 306 9203   AA 0344 209 0754

Condition (body/chassis/interior/mechanicals)

Please read chapter nine for advice on checking the vehicle's general condition, it is there to help you!

All original specification

Modified cars do not appeal to everyone, and you should be aware that they may not be easy to sell later, although some modifications – such as alloy wheels – will be easy to revert back to the original fitments, providing they are still present and in serviceable order. Remember, though, that you may well have to purchase new tyres to go onto them.

Many V8s have had their power outputs boosted by modifications to the engine, which is relatively easy to do as performance parts are plentiful and easily obtained. Common modifications include high-lift camshafts, new inlet and exhaust manifolds, and four-barrel carburettors, all of which will promote more speed; this will not be to everyone's taste, however, as the characteristics of the engine will have changed. Your insurance company may not like it either. A standard car is easier to sell!

Unleaded fuel

All P6s, apart from some low-compression export models, were designed to run on premium fuel (known as five-star in the UK). This is no longer available. Lower-grade fuels can sometimes cause problems with valve seat deterioration, and some cars may have been fitted with hardened valve seats to combat this issue. Many others will have been run using a lead replacement additive in the fuel tank. Both of these methods work very well. However, most cars will not have received any modifications at all, apart, perhaps, from slight retardation of the ignition timing, with no adverse affects whatsoever. If your P6 is going to be subjected to long, high-speed runs, then a lead replacement additive is advisable.

Insurance

Ensure you have some insurance in place, both if you want to test drive a vehicle, and before you collect a car that you have purchased. All P6s should qualify for a 'classic' policy, usually with a limited mileage clause (typically 3000 miles a year). This is often ample for most owners.

How you can pay

The most convenient way to pay for a car these days, especially if buying from a dealer, is by bank transfer before, or at point of, collection. Good, old-fashioned cash is preferred by most private sellers, however.

Buying at auction

Please refer to chapter ten regarding buying at auction.

Professional vehicle check (mechanical examination)

If you are not particularly knowledgeable about car mechanics, then consider having a potential vehicle professionally assessed. The cost of this is relatively small considering the peace of mind it will promote.

| AA | 0800 056 8040 (motoring organisation with vehicle inspectors) |
| RAC | 0330 159 0720 (motoring organisation with vehicle inspectors) |

6 Inspection equipment

– these items will really help

This book!
Reading glasses (if you need them for close work)
A good torch (flashlight)
Overalls or work clothes (you will have to get on the ground)
Digital or mobile phone camera
A knowledgeable friend

A few tips:
• Use this book as a quick reference guide.
• Using a magnet to detect body filler is a little old hat these days. Most body shops use filler to level off panels; filler doesn't necessarily mean rust.
• Using a sharp object to prod and poke the car is not fair to the owner! He will not want you to attack his protective underseal and shiny paintwork with a sharp instrument!
• You will need a torch to inspect the underside properly.
• By all means take a few pictures to use as a reference later, but show the owner the courtesy of asking first.

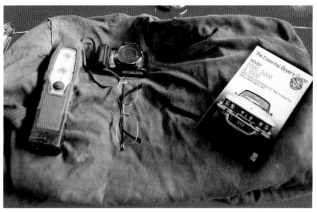

These items will prove invaluable when carrying out a vehicle inspection.

7 Fifteen minute evaluation
– walk away or stay?

There are still plenty of healthy P6s available (at time of writing), which means there is no need to go out and buy the first one you see.

Stand back and take a really good look at the car you have come to view, and form an overall impression in your mind.

Exterior
Does the car sit nicely on the road with no sagging suspension? Are the panels nice and straight? These things are easier to assess when viewing from a few feet away.

From several feet away check that the car sits level. This example sits a little low, indicating slightly worn road springs.

Check for bent or crooked bumpers; this is a common problem with P6s.

Is there any obvious rust? It is unlikely that you will find an original rust-free car, but you may well find one that has had all of its rust issues properly addressed.

Check all of the rubber window seals for perishing.

P6s have a lot of brightwork, but much of it is stainless steel, which is good news as it generally lasts well.

Look for cracks in the leather and splits in the seams. Not all seats will look as good as this.

Check that the car has been fitted with a reputable brand of tyre. If so, this is a good sign that it has been well cared for.

Interior and boot

Check that the spare wheel, jack and wheel brace are present, you'd be surprised how many are missing.

P6 leather interiors can last very well, but if they have not been looked after – the leather kept clean and fed regularly with hide cream – they can deteriorate. The leather itself can split and the stitching can dry out and rot, leaving unsightly open seams.

Velour seats do not generally last well, the cloth often de-laminates and sometimes rots away completely. This problem is not limited to Rover cars, it is an issue associated with velour from the seventies.

Check for holes and discolouration in the headlining and sun visors, the latter often displays deterioration of the inner padding, which results in misshapen visors.

Carpets often show severe signs of wear and/or rotting due to years of condensation or the ingress of water. They are also often badly faded and discoloured. If you are greeted with a strange smell when you open the door it is probably due to rotting carpets. The interior of a P6 should only smell of Connolly leather (unless cloth trim is fitted, of course!).

Velour seats often de-laminate, causing unsightly wrinkles in the cloth, as in this late model 3500S.

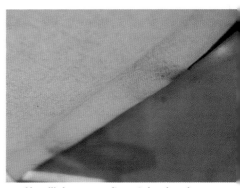

Headlinings are often stained and cleaning can prove difficult.

Don't expect an engine compartment to look brand-new. However, there should be no obvious oil or water leaks, as on this 3500 V8.

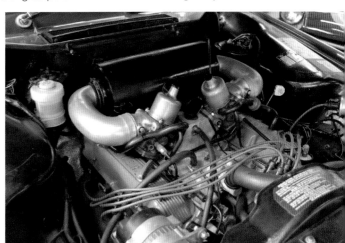

Engine compartment
Don't expect every car to have a super clean engine bay, because very few do, not even show cars. However, there should be no sign of oil or water on or around the engine. Look for shoddily repaired pipes and linkages etc: a sure sign of neglect elsewhere.

Check for anti-freeze stains on the radiator, visible as patches of light green.

All P6s left the factory with their inner wings painted dull black, not the body colour. If you see the latter then the car could have had extensive work done, due to an accident or simply rust.

Paperwork
Only buy a car from an individual who can prove that they are the person named in the car's registration document (V5C in the UK) and, preferably, view and collect the car from the address shown in the document. Check that the registration document refers to the actual car you are looking at! This may seem obvious, but you would be surprised how many people don't notice if they aren't matching.

Don't expect to see a fully-stamped service book from the dealer, as this is rare with a P6.

Road test
Unless your prospective P6 is a restoration case, you must have a road test. Remember, your own insurance policy will not necessarily cover you to drive someone else's car, so, if this is the case, allow the owner to drive.

All P6s, irrespective of what engine is fitted, should be very smooth with absolutely no knocks or groans from the suspension. The steering should be direct with no discernible free-play at the wheel. A fair amount of body roll when cornering is normal on a P6.

Brakes should be excellent on all models.

With manual gearboxes, check that the clutch is light and smooth in operation, with no slippage, and that the gearlever doesn't knock itself into neutral when you jolt your foot on and off the accelerator pedal, especially in reverse (a common problem). On automatics, there should be no heavy knocks when engaging drive or reverse, although a small 'nudge' is normal. There should be no whines or crunching emanating from the gearbox when on the move. Make sure that the car actually drives backwards when reverse is selected, as the loss of reverse gear is a very common fault on automatics. Check that the kickdown mechanism works.

8 Key points

– where to look for problems

Exterior

- Are all the panels straight, with even gaps?
- Is the paint finish and colour consistent?
- Is there any visible rust?
- Is the chrome and brightwork reasonably good, and are the bumpers straight?
- Are the rubber seals in good order?

It would be good if all P6s were as immaculate as this 2000TC. Check for rust, the paint finish, and the panel gaps in particular.

Check the overall condition of the interior, especially the seats. This is the unique rear seat arrangement of the rare estate model.

Interior
- Does the condition of the interior fit the mileage?
- Is the leather cracked and are the stitched seams split?
- Is the velour trim in good condition?
- Have the seats sagged?
- Are the carpets damp or rotten?
- Is the headlining stained?
- Does everything work?

Look for a reasonably clean and well-maintained engine compartment, with no obvious leaks.

Engine and mechanicals
- Is it reasonably clean under the bonnet with just general road dirt?
- Are there any oil or coolant leaks/stains?
- Are the rubber hoses and clips in good condition?
- Is the car sitting level with no signs of sagging suspension?
- Is the car fitted with a decent brand of tyre, are they in date and is there plenty of tread?
- Does the exhaust system sound like it is leaking?
- Are there any bills for mechanical work?

9 Serious evaluation
– 60 minutes for years of enjoyment

Score each section as follows: 4 = excellent; 3 = good; 2 = average; 1 = poor. The totting up procedure is detailed at the end of the chapter. Be realistic in your marking! If you are looking at many cars, it can be difficult to remember the details of each one when the time comes to decide which to purchase. Of course, you may come across a car which instantly stands out amongst the rest, making a decision relatively easy, but, even so, it may prove beneficial to use a scoring system as laid out in this chapter.

A complete inspection is broken down into easy-to-manage sections, each one has its own set of four numbered markers. Complete each inspection process and mark that section accordingly. Try to be realistic and consistent in your marking, and inspect the car in daylight, or in a well lit environment.

Add up the scores when you have completed all the sections and compare it to the guide at the end of the chapter.

General appearance and fit

When you first set eyes on a car you will automatically carry out a quick assessment in your head. It may not necessarily be an accurate one, that is what the individual assessment section of this book is for, but it is a good way to initially assess the car.

Step back and take a really good look from all angles. Does the vehicle look clean, bright and generally well cared for? Does it sit well on the road?

Look for excessive panel gaps, as on this 2000SC: a sure sign that all is not well underneath.

A typically ill-fitting door, in this case due to a poorly-executed rust repair.

Check for the following:
- Ill-fitting panels
- Bent bumpers or trim
- Off-colour panels
- Scrapes and dents
- Torn or tatty trim

Look out for tatty trim; it could be tricky to find replacements.

BODY COLOUR IDENTIFICATION			
ZIRCON BLUE	2 OZ.	1 PINT	1 GALLON
ROVER PART Nos.	366591	366506	366507

The original factory colour is written on this label on the RH inner wing.

Paintwork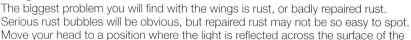

First of all, is the car painted in an original Rover colour? A repaint is to be expected on any car of this age, but a non-factory colour could be difficult to sell later. The original paint colour is clearly written on a label in the engine compartment (with the possible exception of April Yellow).

This car has had its paint colour changed from the original 'Almond' to a non-standard red (actually a Triumph colour), as can be clearly seen by the flaking paint around the door catch.

Check for over-spray on door and window rubbers, bright trim and glass. Poor attention to detail here usually indicates shoddy workmanship elsewhere. Examine the paint finish on every panel closely, checking for a smooth finish without rough 'orange peel,' cracking or fading. Are there any bubbles in the paint? This is a sure sign of hidden rust.

A common problem on cars that have received a cheap repaint is micro-blistering. This is when large areas of paintwork have a covering of tiny micro-bubbles which can often be felt when rubbing the hand across the surface. They can also be seen with the naked eye, though you may have to look very closely. Micro-blisters are bad news, requiring a bare metal repaint to put right.

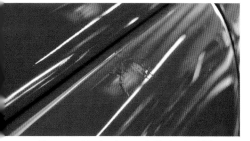

You need to look carefully for bubbles on the wings, as here. Rest assured rust is lurking underneath.

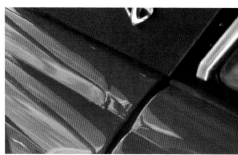

Rear wings tend to break out in rust on the top edge.

Wings and wheelarches

The biggest problem you will find with the wings is rust, or badly repaired rust. Serious rust bubbles will be obvious, but repaired rust may not be so easy to spot. Move your head to a position where the light is reflected across the surface of the panels, then look for ripples or bumps in the paint. This often signifies body filler, which could well be hiding rust.

If the wings appear in excellent condition but have 'fresher' or brighter paint then they could have been replaced – not a bad thing – however, check to see if they are made of steel or fibreglass, this is not always easy to spot. Run your fingers around the inside edge of the wheelarches. Steel will feel smooth with a crisp edge, whilst fibreglass will usually feel a little rough with a textured finish on the back of the panel. Fibreglass panels will reduce a car's value significantly. Common areas of rust are:

Front wings – frontal area (around the side lamp assemblies), rear upper area, lower rear area (next to the sill) and all around the wheelarch.

Rear wings – front edge (especially at the top), below the rear lamps and the lower rear edge.

Doors 4 3 2 1

Again, the biggest issue you will have with the doors is rust. Open them and look at the inside lower edge, this area often rusts away. Whilst you're at it, check the operation of the sliding metal check strap that stops the door from opening too wide. These can fail due to lack of maintenance, causing the door to open up against the adjacent panel, denting it.

Front wings can rust badly at the lower front like this ...

... and at the lower rear such as here.

... and in the corners and along the bottom edge.

Doors tend to rust along this inner edge ...

Doors generally rust along the outside lower edge, especially in the corners. At the time of writing, new 'old stock' door skins are available, but are quite expensive.

Bonnet (hood), boot (trunk) and roof

I have grouped these panels together as they are all made from aluminium and, as such, suffer from different issues to steel. Although aluminium can't actually rust, it does oxidise, which can cause it to crumble away into holes. This is particularly true in areas where the aluminium touches steel (as an electrolytic reaction occurs between the two metals), although this doesn't happen often on P6s. You are more likely to find peeling and flaking paint leaving the bare aluminium exposed, often in very large areas. Bonnets (hoods), in

Although excessive on this example, it does show just how badly the paint can lose its adhesion on aluminium. Also, note the typical parking nudge on the front of the bonnet (hood)!

particular, appear to suffer from this – they also seem to be rather prone to parking nudges!

Front and rear valance and scuttle panels

Both the front and rear valances tend to hold mud, causing corrosion at the ends and along their lower edges.

The front scuttle panel is the one that houses the windscreen wipers and can corrode in all areas, especially where the vent for the heater box pokes through. Check the vent/heater box too, as corrosion here is common.

The rear scuttle panel is the one that houses the fuel filler cap and can corrode at the ends where it meets the rear wings.

Typical rear scuttle rust.

Front scuttle panels and heater air inlets can corrode badly, and heater box replacement is complicated.

Chassis and sills (rockers)

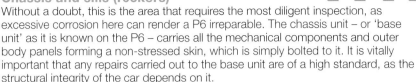

Without a doubt, this is the area that requires the most diligent inspection, as excessive corrosion here can render a P6 irreparable. The chassis unit – or 'base unit' as it is known on the P6 – carries all the mechanical components and outer body panels forming a non-stressed skin, which is simply bolted to it. It is vitally important that any repairs carried out to the base unit are of a high standard, as the structural integrity of the car depends on it.

Much of the base unit cannot be seen with the outer panels attached, but luckily most of the common problem areas are visible as they are underneath the car. You will need to lie on the floor and look carefully where the sills (rockers) fasten

Outer sills are simply screwed to the base unit with self-tappers, and can cover rust, as seen here.

to the floorpan. You will usually see signs of welding here, especially at the ends of the sills, and this is fine as long as the repairs appear to be of a high standard. Check for unsightly welds, excessive underseal and, sadly, even body filler.

The outer sills are secured to the body by simple self-tapping screws, and these should be clearly visible underneath the car. If the sills have been welded to the body instead of screwed, then they are probably hiding a series of horrors: walk away.

Under the bonnet (hood)/boot (trunk) interior

Under the bonnet, inspect the inner wings and the inner panels around the headlamps. Look behind the front wheels and inspect the area around the suspension mountings.

Inside the boot, lift up the trim panels covering the inside of the rear wings and sides of the boot, thus exposing the rear inner wings. You will find quite a large bolt head, one on each inner wing. This is where the rear suspension tie rod bolts

Look for corrosion below the front suspension mountings. Although the front wing is removed in this shot, the area can be clearly seen with the wing in place.

to the main frame of the car. This area corrodes badly, and it is not unusual to find the mounting, complete with bolt, completely torn away, with alarming results to the handling. Do not be surprised to find a welded repair here, which is fine, provided it has been carried out well.

Typical sill-to-floor rust in a poor condition P6. Corrosion as bad as this is usually terminal.

Also check for corrosion in the bottom extremities of the boot floor.

Chrome & bright trim

Look for scratches and marks on the bumpers – this is to be expected, of course, after 40+ years – but the original chrome plating was of high quality, so they should still have a strong lustre.

Expect some minor pitting on all of the chrome plated items: bumpers, lights, door handles, fuel filler cap, etc. The rest of the bright trim is made from stainless steel, and usually retains its finish very well as it is of excellent quality. However, look out for dents in the side rubbing strips on Series II cars.

The bumpers tend to get nudged on their corners causing them to twist. This is surprisingly common, so watch out for it, as good replacements are hard to find.

Wheels, tyres & trims

From the factory, P6s were usually fitted with either Dunlop, Pirreli or Michelin tyres, depending on age and model.

Many cars now have an aftermarket 'Minilite'-style alloy wheel fitted, but note that alloy wheels were never offered, except on some late model V8s, which could be ordered with the innovative (though unsuccessful) Dunlop Safety wheel and Dunlop Denovo run-flat tyres. These are extremely rare now, as they never caught on, and replacement tyres have been unavailable for many years.

Look for a good brand of tyre, such as this Firestone. Note the Minilite style wheel is non-standard.

When buying new tyres for a P6 one doesn't have a lot of choice, as with most older cars, but at least look for a recognised brand, or certainly a good tread pattern. Check the manufacturing date on the sidewall of the tyre.

Don't forget to check the spare and, while you're in that vicinity, check that there's a jack, wheel brace and tool roll, whilst this has no bearing on the car's condition, it's nice to have the original items sitting there.

Glass

The early P6s left the factory with clear glass, and tinted glass became available as an option from 1967. Tinted glass is rare on Series I cars. Check all glass for chips and scratches, especially the windscreen, which could have been damaged, at some point, by badly worn wipers.

Rubber seals

Most of the rubber seals, at over 40 years old, will be cracked and perished to some degree, but consider the cost of replacement if they have ceased to serve their purpose. Front and rear screens can be especially tricky to replace, as they are not fitted in the conventional way.

Side window 'scraper' seals in particular tend to deteriorate badly, resulting in the doors collecting water, which, in turn, causes them to rust away at the bottom.

Note the rubber seals between the doors and wings, and between the doors themselves. Also check the boot and door aperture seals.

Window seals can deteriorate badly, but replacements are available.

At the time of writing, all rubber seals are readily available as reproduction items from specialist suppliers.

General appearance

All P6s were beautifully finished when new, using high quality materials for the most part. Have a good look around the interior, watching out for water stains, torn upholstery and general tidiness. Make sure that everything works; windows, interior lights etc.

Seats & upholstery

The condition of the seats is very important due to the cost of renovation.

There are four basic seat types, each with its own issues:

Early type pleated leather

These are the original design of pleated leather seats as fitted to the P6 from launch; they are very stylish and comfortable. Watch out for leather that is hard and cracked due to lack of proper maintenance and conditioning, and for split and opened up stitching due to the thread rotting. Split stitching is very common, and is not as easy to rectify as you may think.

Hard but sound leather can be softened, to an extent, by treating several times with hide cream, but if it is too hard then, given time, splitting is inevitable. Grubby but sound leather can be cleaned and, if the colour has faded, re-coloured – if done properly, the results are usually excellent.

Look for cracks in the leather, as here.
Note how the colour can fade badly.

Stitching often rots, causing seams to
open up. Repairing this can be tricky.

Box pleat leather

For some reason, these don't seem to wear as well as the earlier, pleated type of seat. The facing often peels away from the leather and, again, the stitching decays.

Box pleat velour

These seats are often fitted to later cars. The velour can separate badly and general decay is common – this is typical of most British Leyland fabrics at the time, as it was a period of cost-cutting across the board. Whilst rear seats are often pristine, the front seats will usually exhibit much more wear, especially the driver's seat.

Vinyl

Some very late cars were fitted with a vinyl version of the box pleat seat. The vinyl often wears through or splits on the front bolsters, sometimes becoming extremely tatty indeed. Replacements are very hard to find.

Oddities

I have seen a few P6s fitted with the early type pleated leather seats, but with the facings upholstered with brushed nylon. These appear to last well, but they are rare.

Door cards, etc

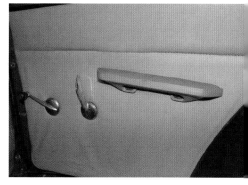

Door cards are made from vinyl-covered fibreboard with a shallow, wood-effect panel running along the top. A few of the very early cars had this panel finished with real wood veneer but these are incredibly rare, most have a mock-wood Formica panel fitted. The use of Formica was an adventurous move by Rover

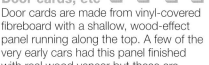

Door cards often deteriorate because of dampness caused by leaking window rubber seals.

at the time; the material was ultra-modern and it gave the P6 cabin a very airy and modern feel. The Formica is very durable and generally lasts well, but do look for splits and other damage due to poor removal over the years.

The door panels themselves often suffer from deterioration of the fibreboard, usually a result of damp caused by leaking window scraper seals. At the time of writing, replacement door panels are available in some colours (black and Buckskin).

Headlining

Look for tears and holes, also for damp stains around the sun visors due to water leaks from the roof aerial. Inspect the sun visors themselves as they can decay inside due to dampness and condensation. There are often stains around the edges of the headlining and also around the central interior light due to ageing of the glue underneath, about which nothing can be done. The glass of the interior light itself often develops a brown stain inside, but removing the glass cover and giving it a good clean in soapy water usually removes this.

Carpets

P6 carpets, especially lighter coloured ones, often turn a grubby brown hue with old age and no amount of cleaning will bring back the original colour. All carpets, irrespective of colour, can fade badly. If there is, or has been, corrosion in the inner sill panels, the carpets in this area will often be badly decayed and rotten, so look out for this. Reproduction carpet sets are available but they are of a different material to the originals.

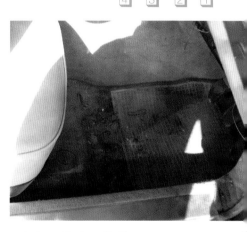

Look for signs of dampness in the carpets, though it may not always be as obvious as this.

Boot interior

P6 boot (trunk) compartments were originally lined in black Rexine – including a cover for the spare wheel, which should be present even with the optional boot mounted spare package. It is always desirable to have the original tool roll complete with tools, even if you never intend to use them.

Reproduction boot linings are available, which are very close to the original in appearance and, if you fancy it, fitted carpet sets are also available.

Check that the boot interior is in good order.

Under the bonnet – first impressions

Any vehicle of this age can be expected to have general road dirt on and around the engine. However, look for a build up of thick, black, old oil due to long periods of leakage, and for fresh oil deposits too. Whilst some oil leaks are relatively simple to fix, others can be expensive, especially if the engine needs to be removed.

With the engine cold, check the water level in the radiator. If it's not filled to the top, then look for leaks. Also, check that there is plenty of anti-freeze in the water, usually indicated by a blue or green colour. P6s rely on anti-freeze as a corrosion inhibitor, so this is important.

Check all the fluid levels under the bonnet. Also check rubber coolant hoses and clips.

Look for coolant leaks on both the front and rear surfaces of the radiator, and also around all the rubber hoses. Leaking coolant usually leaves green stains, especially on the radiator. While you're at it, check the condition of the coolant hoses by squeezing them. The rubber should be firm but flexible. If they are soft and/or cracked they won't last long. Hoses in poor condition with old rusty clips on them indicate a general lack of maintenance that could well mean a lack of attention elsewhere.

Check the water level in the windscreen washer bottle. Again, a lack of attention here could indicate poor maintenance elsewhere.

Unscrew the top from the brake master cylinder and, if it's a manual transmission car, the clutch cylinder. The fluid should be clean in both. If it's dirty then it's yet another sign of poor maintenance.

If the car has automatic transmission, remove the gearbox dipstick and check the level and colour of the fluid. It should be a clean pink or red colour. A dirty brown colour indicates worn bands and clutches meaning a gearbox rebuild is not far away, even though the gearbox may function perfectly (for now ...).

General mechanical issues

When evaluating, just mark the sections relating to the car you are viewing ie four- or eight-cylinder engine and manual or automatic gearbox.

Four-cylinder engines

The four-cylinder engine was considered advanced when it was launched, and was designed specifically for the P6. They can last extremely well if properly maintained.

Although powerful for their size, the four-cylinder unit was never a particularly quiet engine, especially in TC tune – a criticism of the car when new. However, they should pull well and idle smoothly at around 650rpm, a feature Rover prided themselves on. There should be absolutely no squeaks, rattles or knocks of any kind.

A persistent squeak usually indicates a failing water pump or dynamo/alternator bearing. Do not confuse this with a slipping fan belt, which produces a loud squealing noise that gets louder when the engine is revved.

If there is a light tapping noise from the top of the engine, it is usually due to incorrectly adjusted tappets. However, do not underestimate this procedure as it requires removal of the camshaft, expert use of a micrometer and the clearances being adjusted by the removal or addition of shims. Not really a DIY job unless you are a proficient engineer. Also, the adjusting shims would originally have been purchased from a Rover dealer, no longer an option of course, so the shims required could be extremely difficult to find, although you could get them made. Either way, it's a tedious job and it indicates that the engine has been taken apart and incorrectly reassembled – worrying.

Listen for a distinct rattle from the top of the engine when first starting and, possibly, continued rattling on tickover. This is a common problem related to a worn top timing chain. Replacements are readily available and fairly straight forward to fit, if you are a reasonably competent mechanic.

Listen for a blowing exhaust manifold on TC models. These have a tubular steel performance manifold which can crack with age. They can be welded, but removal is necessary to do this. Undamaged replacements are hard to find.

Allow the engine to reach normal operating temperature and check the gauge. The needle should be around half way. If it's higher but the coolant doesn't boil then suspect a partially blocked radiator. If it reads high then drops down again, the thermostat probably needs replacing, which is a simple job. If the needle reads high and stays there, or if the coolant boils, then it is likely to be the cylinder head gasket, which is not so simple.

Many four-cylinder P6s, especially TCs, have a tendency to 'run on,' which means the engine continues to keep running for a short time after you switch off the ignition. This usually only happens when the engine is hot. All P6s were designed to run on five-star premium fuel, which is no longer available. Modern, lower-grade fuels require different ignition and fuel settings to the original factory set up, and, unless they are optimised, 'running on' is a common issue. It can take a skilled hand to accomplish this, but most cars will have been sorted by now. Use premium unleaded petrol, and possibly an octane booster if you car proves problematic in this respect.

V8 engines
Check that the engine runs at normal operating temperature (approximately 85°C). Any variance would indicate similar issues as with the four-cylinder units.

The V8 engine should run and idle very smoothly and quietly. A tapping noise from the top of the engine indicates worn hydraulic tappets. This can often occur when the engine is cold, but should disappear once the engine reaches normal operating temperature. Occasionally, a hydraulic tappet can collapse completely, causing the engine to run unevenly on seven cylinders or less. Hydraulic tappets should be replaced in full sets of 16, and are not too difficult to change, although there is quite a lot of dismantling necessary in order to gain access to them.

Exhaust system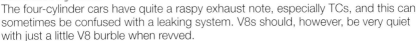
The four-cylinder cars have quite a raspy exhaust note, especially TCs, and this can sometimes be confused with a leaking system. V8s should, however, be very quiet with just a little V8 burble when revved.

Visually check the system for rust and/or repairs, and, on TCs, listen out for a leaking and noisy manifold, as these often crack. Replacements are hard to source.

Full stainless steel exhaust systems for all models (minus manifolds) are readily available at reasonable cost.

Manual transmission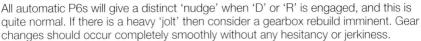
Use this section to assess and score all manual cars.

All P6 manual gearboxes should have a precise action, with all gears engaging easily. Synchromesh should be excellent, with no crunching when changing to a lower gear. Common faults are noisy bearings (evident by a very loud humming sound when slowing down) and the gearlever jumping out of reverse; both mean a gearbox rebuild is required. Gearlevers can also rattle when accelerating, but this is a relatively easy repair, requiring replacement of a bush and/or selector. Note that the V8's manual gearbox is a modified TC unit which, though generally reliable, can wear quickly with heavy use.

Automatic transmission
All automatic P6s will give a distinct 'nudge' when 'D' or 'R' is engaged, and this is quite normal. If there is a heavy 'jolt' then consider a gearbox rebuild imminent. Gear changes should occur completely smoothly without any hesitancy or jerkiness.

Check that the engine will only start in 'P' or 'N.' Have your foot on the brake pedal in case it travels. If there are any issues in this respect then the inhibitor switch on the gearbox is faulty – an easy job to replace.

There should be no vibration from the drivetrain when the car is driven hard. If there is then, again, budget for a gearbox rebuild.

Check that the gearbox fluid is a pink/red colour and that there are no leaks from underneath the car.

Suspension

☐4 ☐3 ☐2 ☐1

All P6s should give an excellent ride at all times, with no clunks or knocks of any kind; indeed, it is one of the car's best features. Although the suspension is quite softly sprung, there should be no bounciness on rough roads. If there is, then suspect worn dampers. However, quite a lot of body roll when cornering is normal.

Check the de Dion rear suspension tube for leaks, as this can be an expensive repair.

Steering

☐4 ☐3 ☐2 ☐1

Cars equipped with power steering should be very easy to turn, with no jerkiness and no noise from the power steering pump. If the power steering pump makes a groaning noise, when the steering is operated with the car stationary and the engine running, a pump rebuild will be necessary. If there is a loud squealing noise from the pump when the steering is turned, then suspect little more than a worn or loose belt.

Non-power steering cars will obviously require more effort to turn the steering wheel, but not overly so. Once on the move, steering should be light and easy to use.

If the car is a little vague when travelling in a straight line, then suspect worn or incorrectly adjusted front wheel bearings. Incorrectly inflated tyres can also cause similar problems. There should be absolutely no free play at the steering wheel.

Brakes

☐4 ☐3 ☐2 ☐1

All P6 brakes, even the very early cars equipped with the Dunlop system, should be powerful in operation with no judder or squealing. The car should pull up squarely and quickly when braking heavily in a straight line.

The handbrake should be efficient in operation, if it's not then expect a full rear calliper rebuild – a complex job on a P6, due to the onboard rear disc system.

Professional evaluation

If you are really unsure what you are looking at, then consider getting a professional inspection for peace of mind. A little money spent at this stage could save you an awful lot later on.

Evaluation procedure

Add up all of the points you have marked, remembering to only score the engine and transmission applying to the car being examined.

Score:
25-50   Poor condition, in need of much work. Are you sure?
50-75   Average car, some work needed but could be roadworthy and usable.
75-100   Good to excellent. Smart and presentable, possibly show standard.

10 Auctions
– sold! Another way to buy your dream

Auction pros & cons
Pros:
• Prices can sometimes be lower than those of a dealer, so you might get a bargain on the day.
• You will have plenty of opportunity to examine the car and the paperwork.

Cons:
• You cannot drive the car.
• Auction cars often need work, and you won't know how much until you get it home.
• It is easy for a private buyer (as opposed to a dealer) to pay too much.
• There is usually no guarantee whatsoever. If you win the car, then you own it come what may.
• There will usually be a buyers premium to pay on top of the hammer price and many private buyers forget this.

Which auction?
Auctions by established auctioneers are advertised in car magazines and on the auction houses' websites. Although a printed catalogue may only be available a few days before the auction, the lots are usually listed with photographs on the auctioneers' website much earlier. Also, previous auction prices are often available online.

Catalogue, entry fee and payment details
When you purchase the auction catalogue, it often acts as a ticket for two people to gain entry on the day. Catalogue details tend to be brief, but will include information such as "one owner from new," "full service history" etc. It will also give a guide price for each lot, giving you some indication of what you will need to pay, though this is by no means always accurate. Buyers premium will be published also, so ensure you remember to add this to the estimates. The catalogue will inform you of the various methods of accepted payment. Cars are not normally released before full payment is made, and, if this is delayed, storage charges may apply.

Viewing
You will usually have ample chance to view the auction lots – from several days before the auction, right up until the point of sale – so don't waste the opportunity. There will be auction staff available to assist you by allowing access under the bonnet, inside the boot and interior etc. Staff will also start the car for you but a test drive is usually not permitted. And, whilst you will be able to crawl underneath the car as much as you wish, you will not be permitted to jack it up. Any available paperwork relating to the car will be available for inspection via the auction office.

Bidding
Before you take part in the auction, decide on the maximum you want to pay (don't forget the buyers premium) and stick to that price. It is very easy for the inexperienced to get carried away by 'auction fever' and pay over the odds.

It may be several hours before the car that you are interested in appears, so make good use of the time to establish who is bidding, and on what. It will soon become apparent who the traders are, and what sort of cars they are after. Watch from the way they bid and learn from it. When 'your' car comes along, make an early bid as this will alert the auctioneer that you are interested, it is extremely annoying when you make a bid at the last minute and the auctioneer doesn't see you! Let the auctioneer know if you have reached your maximum bid by clearly shaking your head and miming "NO."

If the car doesn't make its reserve price, it may still be possible to come to a compromise after the auction by expressing further interest at the auction office. In fact, many lots are sold this way.

Successful bid
If you are the winning bidder there are further things to consider. To get the car home, you will need to arrange insurance and road tax or, alternatively, transport by trailer or transporter. You must have all of these things in hand before you bid!

eBay & other online auctions
eBay and other online auctions may get you a car at a bargain price, but never bid for a vehicle unless you have made the journey to inspect it. Photographs can be, and usually are, very deceptive. Also, some sellers use false or old photographs that in no way resemble the car listed. Always remember, if something appears too good to be true, then it usually is.

Auctioneers
Barrett-Jackson www.barrett-jackson.com
Bonhams www.bonhams.com
British Car Auctions (BCA) www.bca-europe.com or www.british-car-auctions.co.uk
Christie's www.christies.com
Coys www.coys.co.uk
eBay www.eBay.com
HandH www.classic-auctions.co.uk
RM Sotheby's www.rmsothebys.com
Shannons www.shannons.com.au
Silver www.silverauctions.com

11 Paperwork
– correct documentation is essential!

Classic and prestige cars often come with a folder full of paperwork accrued over the years, and this represents the true history of the vehicle. Careful examination will paint an accurate picture of how that vehicle has been maintained and the level of care it has received.

Receipts from specialists are good news, especially if there are several from the same one as they will know the car well. Also, they can probably help with any enquiries you may have about the state of the car. However, many beautifully restored cars may have no written record of their earlier lives at all, but there should be at least some evidence of the restoration costs.

Registration documents

All countries have some form of written confirmation of ownership, and this should ideally be in the vendor's name. If it is not, then politely ask why, there may be a perfectly valid reason (sale due to bereavement for example). By contrast, a dealer will usually **not** have a registration document in his name, it will still be in the name of the previous owner. In the UK, a dealer can log the vehicle with the DVLA without changing the details on the registration document.

If the vehicle has a foreign registration number and document it can usually be re-registered in your name, but this could be a lengthy process and, in some cases, a costly one.

Previous ownership records

Due to the introduction of important new legislation on data protection, it is no longer possible to acquire, from the British DVLA, a list of previous owners of a car you own, or are intending to purchase. This scenario will also apply to dealerships and other specialists, from whom you may wish to acquire information on previous ownership and work carried out.

Roadworthiness certificate

Most countries require some kind of regular test to establish a vehicle's general roadworthiness, so ask to see it. One exception is the UK where, at the time of writing, a vehicle aged 40 years or more from the first date of registration no longer has to have a certificate of roadworthiness (MOT), although many owners continue with the annual test.

In the UK all MOT information since the year 2000 is recorded in computerised archives and is readily accessible to the public online. This is useful in establishing a car's previous failings and mileage.

Road licence

Just about every country implements some form of road taxation. If you intend to drive a vehicle from one country to another, you will need to check the legislation relating to all of the countries through which you will be driving. Note that, in the UK, road tax is not transferable from one owner to the next, so you will have to re-tax the vehicle in your name before you can legally drive it on a public road. Note also that road tax is free for all vehicles aged 40 years or more from the first date of registration.

In the UK, vehicles which are not taxed must be 'SORNed' (be subject to a 'Statutory Off-Road Notification') and this is also not transferable to a new owner: a new SORN must be registered with the DVLA. If this is not done quickly, you could well be issued with a hefty fine.

The car's VIN is on this plate under the bonnet ...

... check it against the registration document and any old MOTs, etc.

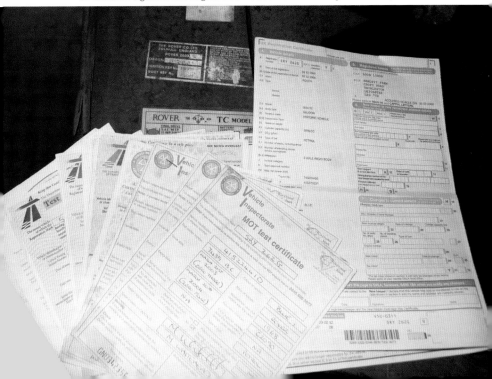

12 What's it worth?
– let your head rule your heart

Condition

Unless you are looking specifically for a P6 to restore, use the scoring system to help you ascertain into which category your car falls; poor-average, average-good or good-excellent. Cars which are beyond excellent (ie as-new or concourse), can achieve much higher prices, and you must decide how much you are prepared to pay for such a car, as there are no price guides that take them into account. Most cars, however, will fit into one of the three price groups:

At the time of writing, condition three cars range from approximately x800 to ●x2500, condition two from ●x2500 to ●x4000, and condition one from ●x4000 to ●x6500. Really excellent cars can cost between ●x10,000 and ●x14,000, and as-new, rebuilt V8s as much as ●x20,000.

Generally speaking, a V8 model will make more than a four-cylinder car in comparable condition and, of the four-cylinder cars, a TC will cost more than an SC. Likewise, a manual transmission car will usually cost more than an automatic.

Desirable options/extras

Some P6 owners strive to locate and fit every available factory extra to their car, but this is not to everyone's taste. However, cars fitted out in this manner do tend to make a little more money than those with a more standard specification. Sadly, many owners of these high-specification cars tend to over-value them.

Factory options can include:
- Power steering
- Full length sunroof
- Sliding steel sunroof (rare)

Full-length sunroof is a desirable option.
Sliding steel sunroofs were also offered, but are extremely rare.

- Mock wood-rim steering wheel and gearlever knob (rare)
- Boot mounted spare wheel kit
- Air-conditioning
- 'Icelert' ice warning system
- Tinted glass
- Front and rear headrests
- Wire wheels (Series I, rare)

The fake wood-rim steering wheel is a rarely seen option offered on Series I cars.

This badge signifies that the optional boot-mounted spare wheel kit is fitted, though not in use on this occasion. The badge is removed and the wheel bolted to the boot lid in its place.

The 'Icelert' ice detector, an extremely rare option on UK cars, though often fitted to export models.

The early type of front headrests seen here ...

... and the later type, here.

Rear headrests were an option which were rarely fitted.

North American export models were fitted with these bonnet ducts, sometimes replicated on UK cars, although they were never a factory option in the UK.

Wire wheels were an option on Series I cars only ...

... whilst these chrome Rostyles were the option for Series II cars.

13 Do you really want to restore?
– it'll take longer and cost more than you think

If you are buying a P6 to restore, you will need to consider who is going to do the work and what it will cost. If you can do most of the work yourself, then costs can be kept to a minimum, but if you need to contract out the work to specialists then things can (make that **will** ...) get expensive. Either way, the cost will certainly outweigh the value of the car at current P6 values.

Think carefully before taking on a restoration project ...

So why restore at all? If you are a competent restorer it may be the perfect, or only, way you can have the exact specification of P6 to suit your needs and desires. You will have the final choice of colour, interior, equipment, everything. Also, you will be assured of the standard of work which has gone into its restoration. In effect, you can build yourself a 'new' P6, with the exact

... it could take longer and cost more than you think.

options you would have chosen at the dealer if you'd have bought a new one back in the day.

If you do decide to buy a P6 to restore, be very wary of incomplete cars. Any missing parts may be extremely difficult to replace, hence why they are missing.

Restoration negatives:
• Do not underestimate just how bad a car might be under the surface.
• Do not underestimate how much other people's services might cost!
• Unless you are experienced, don't take on too much, good restoration work usually takes longer and costs more than most people think. It is easy to run out of interest (and money).
• Beware restoration projects with missing parts as some may be impossible to find.

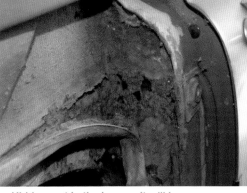

Hidden rust in the base unit will be your biggest problem if restoring.

Restoration positives:
• Rebuilding a car could be the answer to owning the 'perfect' P6 that you cannot find for sale, and you will know exactly the standard of work that has gone into it.
• You can build it to your own specification.
• Restoration costs can be spread over time to suit your budget.
• Restoring can be great fun and immensely satisfying.
• You will be saving another P6 from the breaker's yard.

Excellent interior and a very low mileage make this car a practical candidate for restoration.

When new, all P6s were finished, to a high standard, in cellulose paint. It is unlikely that you will find a P6 with its original paint finish in a serviceable condition, therefore you will probably be looking for faults in an old (or even not so old ...) repaint. These are the problems most encountered:

Orange peel
This means the paint finish has a texture resembling the skin of an orange, with tiny dimples all over its surface. This is caused by unskilled application and would indicate that the rest of the preparation work is also sub-standard. A fresh repaint is the only real answer.

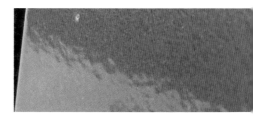

Peeling
Peeling paint means poor adhesion due to bad preparation before a previous respray. This often occurs at the edge of panels where the old paint has not received adequate sanding. The only answer is to start again and carry out a fresh repaint.

Cracking
Cracking of the paint finish is usually caused by poor preparation and/or prolonged exposure to extreme weather conditions. Cars coming from a hot climate often have cracked paint. The only solution is a bare metal respray.

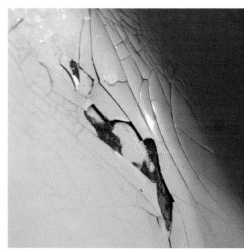

Crazing
A 'crazed' paint finish, similar to cracking (described above), is usually caused by previous poor preparation. Again, a bare metal respray is required.

Cracked and peeling paint mean a bare metal respray is needed.

Blistering
Blisters or bubbles in the paint finish are usually caused by rust on the metal underneath. Very large blisters or bubbles indicate lifting body filler, again, ultimately caused by underlying rust. Effective repair usually means replacing the affected panel.

Micro blistering

Micro blistering is when large areas of paint (often the whole car) are covered with microscopic bubbles resembling a rash. These are often simply sanded smooth and painted over, which looks good for a short time, but, in all cases, the bubbles return. The long-term solution is to carry out a bare metal respray.

Fading

All old paint fades, to a degree, if not polished regularly. If the fading is not severe then rebuffing with a polishing compound will restore the colour and shine. However, this is not always effective. Sometimes the old paint finish simply will not respond, or, if it does, it might not always last. If the previous faded finish returns, the car will need a respray.

Dimples, or silicones

A paint surface covered with small indentations resembling dimples is usually caused by wax residue or silicone traces under the paint. 'Silicones' are a painters worst nightmare, and if they are present it is almost impossible to remove them, a bare metal respray is usually the only solution.

Dents

Don't be too worried by small dents, as specialist companies such as Dent Master can often remove them without the need to re-paint anything, and at a very reasonable cost.

Micro blistered paint can just be seen on the roof pillar of this 3500S Estate.

15 Problems due to lack of use

– just like their owners, P6s need exercise!

The majority of classic cars would benefit from a lengthy drive every few weeks, in the summer months at least. No one, of course, likes to take their beloved classic out in the winter, and that's perfectly understandable; but it should be stored correctly, with the engine started at regular intervals and allowed to reach normal operating temperature. If, however, a car is in storage for most of the time, year in and year out, then unexpected problems can arise; this is why very low mileage cars can prove troublesome when they are pressed into regular use after long periods of not being driven.

Seized components

The components that tend to seize with lack of use are brake callipers, master and slave cylinders, handbrake mechanisms, and the clutch plate. In severe cases the engine itself can seize too.

Brake components can corrode due to lack of use; this being the extreme.

Even brake callipers that appear sound can corrode inside the piston bore due to lack of use.

Fluids

All fluids in a classic car (in fact any car) should be renewed every two or three years, irrespective of mileage covered, and this also applies to air-conditioning refrigerant.

Anti-freeze loses its anti-corrosion abilities over time, sometimes with catastrophic results. Core plugs can rust through or pop out due to freezing coolant in the winter; engine blocks can crack and water passages can corrode, rendering an engine scrap. Sadly, some of these issues can develop over a period of time, and may go unnoticed until a major failure occurs.

A common issue on cars that have been unused for long periods is a build up of silt in the engine waterways and radiator, which often results in the engine running hot. However, a good quality coolant flush, together with a new radiator, usually solves the problem.

Brake fluid, with the exception of the silicone variety, naturally absorbs water, which causes it to partially lose its hydraulic capabilities. The particles of water in the brake lines and callipers cause the pistons to corrode, which, in turn, tears the rubber seals. This also applies to the clutch hydraulic system. Even though the pedal can feel perfectly firm and normal, heavy braking can trigger loss of brakes as the fluid boils. These issues are due to water in the lines. Brake fluid should be changed every two years.

Fuel system

Modern fuels do not fair well when they get a little old, turning to a wax-like substance that will not ignite. It also clogs up the carburettors, fuel pump, fuel lines and fuel tank, all of which could be surprisingly costly to rectify.

Exhaust system

All exhaust systems, even stainless steel ones, rust from the inside; this is due to trapped condensation caused by the exhaust gases. On cars that are seldom used, the resultant corrosion can have quite an alarming effect on the system, with rust holes appearing just about everywhere.

Tyres

Tyres that have been immobile for long periods will often vibrate badly once pressed into use again. This usually improves, or even disappears completely, with constant use, but not always.

Old tyres perish and rot, often causing the side walls to collapse at speed. Even if the tyres have plenty of tread on them, always check the date of manufacture (cast into the rubber on the side wall). If more than five years old they should be renewed as a safety precaution, even if they have covered very little mileage.

Check tyres for cracked sidewalls and the date of manufacture, which is usually cast into the rubber.

The distorted seats in this 2000TC indicate that it has been stored in damp conditions. Examine the rest of the car carefully.

Rubber and plastic parts

Radiator hoses may have perished and split due to lack of use, resulting in a total loss of the all important anti-corrosive coolant. Window rubbers can harden and leak. Gaiters, boots and grommets can crack and split. Wiper blades will harden and split.

Interior trim

Leather seats will harden and crack if not treated with hide food regularly (at least twice a year). Velour upholstery will de-laminate with lack of use and the fabric will fade if exposed to sunlight. Condensation will affect all carpets and trim badly.

Battery

It is unlikely the battery will be serviceable if the car has not been used regularly. Electrical connectors, especially earth connections (grounds) oxidise over time and lose their conductive properties, which can cause all manner of peculiar electrical issues. Wiring can become hard and brittle, often causing short circuits and even fires.

Batteries will soon die if a car is not driven regularly unless a trickle charger is used.

16 The Community
– key people, organisations and companies in the P6 world

Clubs
Rover P6 Owners' club www.p6roc.co.uk
Rover P6 Club www.p6club.com

**For help and support from other enthusiasts join a club!
It will prove extremely beneficial.**

Parts and accessories
JR Wadhams,
The Brads Nail Works,
45 Valley Road,
Lye,
Stourbridge,
West Midlands
DY9 8JG
www.jrwadhams.co.uk
01384 891800

Wins International Ltd.,
Unit 21B, Durkins Road,
Charlwoods Industrial Estate,
East Grinstead,
West Sussex
RH19 2ER
www.winsintltd.co.uk
01342 327018

MGBD Parts,
Unit 1, Ashford Industrial Estate,
Dixon Street,
Wolverhampton,
WV2 2BX
roverp6parts.com
01902 689975

Specialists
Kingsdown Garage,
Unit 21, Pioneer Road,
Faringdon,
Oxfordshire
SN7 7BU
01367 244646

Ankerbold Garage,
Unit 4, Ankerbold Road,
Chesterfield
S42 6BU
01264 860860

MH Annable & Son,
Unit 20, Darley Abbey Mills,
Darley Abbey,
Derby
DE22 1DZ
01332 346299

Useful books
Rover P6 1963-1977 by James Taylor

17 Vital statistics
– essential data at your fingertips

Production figures

Model	Number built	
2000	99,926	
2000 Auto	27,909	
2000TC	68,486	
2200SC	9929	
2200SC Auto	6115	
2200TC	16,905	
3500	62,256	
3500S	16,825	
3500S Fed	2043	These figures include all UK and export cars

Technical specifications

Model	Production period	Engine capacity	Configuration	Peak power (bhp) @ rpm	Max torque (lb/ft) @ rpm
2000	64-73	1978cc	4-cyl OHC	99SA@5000 89DIN@5000	121SAE@3600 108DIN@2500
2000TC	67-73	1978cc	4-cyl OHC	124SAE@5500 109DIN@5500	132SAE@4000 124DIN@2750
2000SC	74-77	2205cc	4-cyl OHC	98DIN@5000	126DIN@2500
2200TC	74-77	2205cc	4-cyl OHC	115DIN@5000	135DIN@3000
3500	68-76	3528cc	8-cyl OHV	184SAE@5200 144DIN@5000	226SAE@3000 202DIN@2700
3500S	72-76	3528cc	8-cyl OHV	144DIN@5000	202DIN@2700

Performance figures

Model	Max speed (mph)	Acceleration 0-60mph (secs)	50-70mph in top gear	Average fuel consumption	Kerb weight (lb)
2000	102	15.1	13.6	24	2804
2000TC	107	11.9	12.3	25	2851
2000 Auto	94	18	18	21	2885

Model	Max speed (mph)	Acceleration 0-60mph (secs)	50-70mph in top gear	Average fuel consumption	Kerb weight (lb)
2000SC (S2)	102	14.7	15.1	25	2804
2000TC (S2)	105	12.2	12.5	22	2946
2200 SC	101	13.4	11.5	27	2822
2200SC Auto	101	14.5	12.3	20	2867
2200TC	107	11.4	12.2	21	2887
3500 (S1)	114	10.5	9.2	17	2946
3500 (FED)	117	11.9	N/A	17	3195
3500 (S2)	112	10.8	8.8	19	2979
3500S	122	9.1	8.3	20	2979

Dimensions

Length	179 inches	4547mm
Width	66 inches	1676mm
Height	55.2 inches	1403mm
Wheelbase	103.5 inches	2630mm

The Essential Buyer's Guide™ series ...

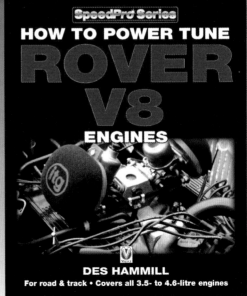